Don't Read This Book, Whatever You Do!

MORE POEMS ABOUT SCHOOL

KALLI DAKOS

ILLUSTRATED BY
G. BRIAN KARAS

ISBN 0-590-16256-X

Text copyright © 1993 by Kalli Dakos.
Illustrations copyright © 1993 by G. Brian Karas.
All rights reserved. Published by Scholastic Inc., 555 Broadway,
New York, NY 10012, by arrangement with Simon & Schuster Books
for Young Readers, a division of Simon & Schuster, Inc.
TRUMPET and the TRUMPET logo are registered trademarks of
Scholastic Inc.

12 11 10 9 8 7 6 5 4 3 2 1   6 7 8 9/9 0 1/0

Printed in the U.S.A.

The text of this book is set in Sabon.
The illustrations are rendered in pencil on paper.

This book is for my mother,
Betty Sperdakos, and for
the students and teachers
who are my inspiration
—K.D.

For Sara and Evan
—G.B.K.

Contents

I Gotcha

I gotcha,
I caughtcha,
I putcha
In my poem.

I lockedcha,
Forever,
In my poetry zone.

If You're Not Here, Then Where Are You?

MS. JONES: If you're not here, please raise your hand.

(Hands go up everywhere.)

MS. JONES: If you're not here, *then where are you?*

SYLVIA: I'm miles and seasons from here today,
        Playing on a beach a summer away.

KATHY: I'm riding a comet through outer space,
        Winning first prize in a galactic race.

ALEX: I'm lying in bed on a cloud of dreams,
        Floating over valleys of whipping cream.

SARAH: I'm on a planet that's so terribly cool,
        No homework, no tests, no report cards, no
        school.

NICK: I'm not here, even though I am,
        Come with me, Ms. Jones, if you can.

MS. JONES: By a fresh mountain stream, I'll go and rest,
        Worlds away from the work on my desk.

Best Friends

Your work is neat; mine's such a mess.
I rush too much; you do your best.

You get straight *A*'s; I get all *C*'s.
I'm Tom Sawyer; you're Socrates.

You love library; I race to gym.
I'm elastic; you're a straight pin.

You're a violin; I'm a tambourine.

But we're the best friends
This school has ever seen.

The Star

Tonight,
I'll wait until
The sun has finished
His homework
And gone to bed.
Then I'll tiptoe outside
And climb
My apple tree.

From the highest branch
I will search the night
For my special star.

I will pluck
It from the sky
As if it were an apple
On my tree.

Then I'll put it in my pocket,
And keep my secret
Hidden
Until our spelling test.

Tomorrow,
When my teacher
Gives out the stars
To all the good spellers,
I won't be sad,
Because I'll have
One, too.

Eric Is Allergic to Girls

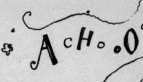

NARRATOR: Eric began to make a fuss
When Jane sat by him on the bus,
First he coughed, then he wheezed,
Then he blew a monstrous sneeze.

ERIC: I always get sick when I sit near you,
I think I'm allergic to girls. *Ah-chooooooooo!*

JANE: Your brain must be the size of a dot,
To have such a silly, stupid thought.

ERIC: My face is red, and starting to burn,
I *am* allergic to you and your germs.

JANE: There's no such thing as allergic to girls,
There's no such thing in the whole wide world.

ERIC: You lie! You lie! You certainly do,
I am allergic to girls like you.
I cough, I sneeze, I choke, I wheeze,
And sometimes I can hardly breathe.
I'm sitting here in misery,
So get your germs away from me.

JANE:	I see you cough, I watch you sneeze,
	I hear you choke, I feel you wheeze,
	But I won't move from this seat,
	Even if moss grows on my feet,
	And your nose turns a fiery red,
	And a hundred spots bloom on your head.
	No boy in the entire world
	Has ever been allergic to girls.
NARRATOR:	Then Jane let out a shocking sneeze,
	And in a massive, swirling breeze,
	Eric blast into the air,
	Through the window, gone somewhere,
	And Jane yelled as upward he flew,
JANE:	*I'm allergic to boys like you!*

12

You Were Hatched in a Witch's Brew

MEAN STUDENT:
Laughing at Kate

You're so ugly you belong in a zoo,
The clothing you wear is hideous, too,
You must have been hatched in a witch's brew.

KATE:
Smiling

Some of the things you say are true,
I *was* hatched in a witch's brew,
Now watch me cast a spell on you!

Poof!

MEAN STUDENT:

Ribbit! Ribbit!

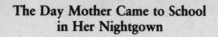

The Day Mother Came to School in Her Nightgown

It was the most gloomy, dismal sight,
As if the dark had stolen the light,

The winds were all blowing around the town,
When Mother came to school in her nightgown.

It was a mistake, I know it's true,
For it wasn't what she meant to do,

But when she kissed me by the door,
The winds locked it shut with a roar.

"I'll find a neighbor," my mom said,
"Who's not at work and not in bed,

"To help me make my way back in,
Before the stormy rains begin."

Together we walked down the street,
Oh, life can be so bittersweet,

For then a crash of thunder came,
The sky lit in a brilliant flame.

Then it turned a shadowy gray,
Till beams of light came our way.

The school bus rumbled down the street,
But before it stopped at our feet,

The rain came rushing all around,
An entire cloud came gushing down,

And when the bus doors opened fast,
We climbed inside, my mom was last.

"I will have to ride this bus to school,
Or be wetter than a swimming pool,"

She said as she sat down near Joe.
This is all true, I tell you so.

When we arrived at school we dashed,
Through the doors as quick as a flash,

And when I looked around to see,
My mom was standing right by me.

I turned red when my friends found,
My mother there in her nightgown.

"Hello, Ms. Smith," a teacher said,
"You look like you should be in bed."

"Why did I get out of bed today?"
My mom said, looking an ashen gray.

"In the office, I'll phone a cab,
Or maybe try and reach your dad."

Into the office I watched her go,
This is all true, I tell you so.

When the winds were blowing around the town,
My mother came to school in her nightgown.

Herstory = Her Story

You can study history,
While I study herstory,
*His*tory,
*Her*story,
Whose will it be?

Voices from the Lost and Found

"I miss her so much,"
The neon shoelace cried
To the purple pencil.
"Do you think Sarah,
My sweetheart,
Will forget about me?"

"I guess it depends
How long you're here,"
Sighed the pencil,
Gazing at the dull brown walls
Of the lost-and-found box.
He continued,
"I used to hate it when
My owner brought me to school
In his stuffy pencil case,
With old pieces of gum
And dirty lunch money.
But now I'd give anything
To be home again."

"Will someone please tell
Those mittens to stop crying,"
Bellowed the ruler.
"I am fed up with their tears.
I do hope spring is in the air,
So we won't have any more
Hysterical mittens to deal with."

"Spring!" yelled the baseball cap.
"I hope it *is* time for spring.
Sun shining.
Three bases,
Pitcher,
Batter,
That's home for me.
I *know* my owner
Will miss me
If it's spring."

"My owner will *never* miss me,"
Sighed the underwear.
"He has sixteen pairs
Exactly like me—
With stegosauri
All over them."

"How did a kid lose his underwear?"
Asked the teddy bear.

"It was on a class trip
To a swimming pool,"
Explained the underwear.
"My dopey owner
Took so long
Getting out of the water
That he didn't
Have time to change,
And had to wear
His *wet* bathing suit home.

He left *me* lying on the floor
In the locker room.
Luckily, a teacher found me
And brought me back to school."

"I wish those two mittens
That don't match
Would stop crying
For their twins,
So we could get some rest,"
Interrupted the toilet-bowl eraser.
"I suppose I'm the only one
Who likes it here."

"How can you possibly
Like it here?"
Asked the underwear.

"If you were in the shape
Of a toilet bowl,
You might understand,"
He sighed.
"Out there,
In the classrooms,
I'm just a gag—
A joke to laugh at,
Like a kid who gets
Every spelling word wrong,
Or a substitute teacher
Who can't control the class."

Thump! Thump! Thump!

"Shhhhhhhhhhh!"
Warned the baseball cap.
"I hear someone
Coming toward our box.
You'd better all duck!"

PLOP!

"Ouch!
Get off of me,"
Bellowed the ruler.
"Why are you rolling
Around like that?"

A squeaky voice replied,
"I'm a roll
Of paper.
Where am I?"

"You're in the
Lost-and-found box,"
Replied the underwear.
"What kind of paper
Are you, anyway? "

"I'm a notepad,
In the shape of toilet paper.
Oh, go ahead and laugh,
Everyone else does!"

"I would *never* laugh,"
Interrupted the eraser.
"Never! Ever! Ever!"

The notepad rolled
Closer to the eraser
And exclaimed,
"Hooray!
I think I've *finally*
Found a friend!"

Dear Brothers and Sisters

Dear Brothers and Sisters,
(Red, green, blue, yellow, pink, black,
brown, white, and orange pencils)

Three days ago,
I fell onto the floor
Under the guinea-pig cage.
The janitor swept me up
In a pile of dirt,
And put me in the garbage can
Beside a rotten apple core,
And a green sock
That smelled like
A sick skunk.

I was ready to throw up
When the teacher saw me,
And put me in the
Lost-and-found box.

I've been here for three days,
And I've met a lot of great friends—
My favorite is
An eraser that is shaped
Like a toilet bowl.

We are trying to keep our spirits up,
But it is hard because
Two mittens that don't match
Are always crying
For their twins.

I will be as brave
As a student
Who tickles a bully,
And I will keep writing
Until I am found.

Yours truly,
Purple Pencil

P.S. Please write me.

I Live for Gym

I
live
for
gym
I
breathe
for
gym
I
watch
the
clock
and
race
to
gym

I'm
free
in
gym
to
run
and
play
to
try
new
games
and
shout
"Hooray!"

It's
in
the
gym
I
feel
so
good
I'd
live
there
if
I
only
could

Have
gym
the
whole
day
through
why
then
I'd
always
dash
to
school

GYM
SWEE
GYM

Cures for a Boring School Day

Invent a new toy.

Weigh cotton candy.

Go on an insect safari.

Write a letter to Donald Duck or Goofy.

Eat jellybean sandwiches and candy-apple soup.

Turn your classroom into a theater and act out poems.

Compete in the First Annual Bubble-Gum-Blowing Olympics.

Are You Sleeping?
Is It Clear?

MR. COPIS TO CLASS:

Fold your paper right in two,
Then color one side dark blue.
Cut an inch and a half
Off one end,
Then draw an octagon
With your pen.
Take your scissors,
Cut right here . . .

Are you sleeping?

Is it clear?
Is it clear?
Is it clear?

MR. COPIS TO HIMSELF:

(*Now it's time to check and see*
Which students listen to me.)

MR. COPIS TO CLASS:

Take the paper once again.
Chew a big bite off the end.

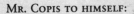

ALBERTO:

I fold my paper right in two,
And color one side dark blue.
I cut an inch and a half
Off one end,
And draw an octagon
With my pen.
I take my scissors,
Cut right here,
All instructions
Are crystal clear.
I chew a big bite off the end . . .

Why are we eating paper again?

A Fourth Grader's Secret

I have a secret,
Terrible and true,
Locked in my crayons
And workbooks, too,
Come closer
So I can whisper
To you!

I haven't raised my hand,
Since I was in grade two!

An Ode to a Toe

My teacher says
To write a poem,
About anything
I want.
Should I write about
A river or a rose,
A finger or a toe?

That's it!

I'll write an ode to my toe.

Here I go!

I love you toe,

I really do,

You're always there
inside my shoe.

You know,
Toe,
If I were Juliet,
You'd be my
Romeo

You know,
Toe,
You came free,
Didn't cost any dough
You tag along
Wherever I go,
You grew with me,
Nice and slow,
And I just thought
You'd like to know
You're Special,
Toe!

Something Splendid

David ripped
Two legs from
A daddy longlegs
He found on the playground.
The legs shook
For a few minutes,
And then stopped forever.

David smiled
Like a lizard,
And when I wasn't looking,
He put those legs
On my desk
And waited for me to
scream.

But I didn't.

I looked at those legs
And imagined
How just this morning
They worked
With six other legs,
On a body
That snuggled so close
To the ground
It could probably hear
The earth's heartbeat.

That daddy longlegs
Could see
And hear
And feel,
And maybe even think,
Or dream
About a world
We can't even imagine.

If David worked
His entire lifetime,
He probably
Couldn't make
Something . . .

As splendid!

Pick Me, Please

Teacher
Teacher
Pick me please
I know the name
Is Hercules

Ask me
Ask me
Just this once
I'll prove to you
I'm not a dunce

My hand
My hand
Is waving high
Won't you catch it
With your eye

My heart
My heart
Is beating fast,
Just waiting
For you to ask . . .

Me?
You picked me?
Wow!
Me!

The answer . . .
Um . . .
Uh . . .
Oh . . .
Ot . . .

I think . . .

I think . . .

I just forgot!

Dreams Brewing

Gum chewing

Noses blowing   Bodies wiggling

Rulers sliding

Papers rustling   Pencils tapping

Chalk scratching

ongues wagging   Feet scuffling   Chairs rocking

Minds cruising
Pens striking   Thoughts jumping
Views forming
Pages turning   Hopes growing

Dreams brewing.

Where Dreams Don't Cry

MS. FREEMAN:

Naomi,
You're lost in dreams today,
Tell me,
    Tell me,
        Where do you stray?

NAOMI:

A galaxy far from our Milky Way,
I'm journeying,
    journeying,
        there today.

Where stars shine forever
And dreams don't cry,
And our grandfathers
Never
    ever
        die.

I'd Mark with the Sunshine

If I were a teacher,
I wouldn't mark in red,
Because red reminds me
Of blood that
Oozes out of cuts,
And fire engines that
Rush to fight blazes
So hot you could
Die in them,
And STOP signs that
Warn you of danger.

If I were a teacher
I'd mark in yellow—
For corn muffins,
Mustard on a fat hot dog,
Gardens of dandelions,
And sunbeams that
Dance on daffodils.

If I were a teacher,
I'd throw out
My STOP pen,
*And I'd mark with
The sunshine itself!*
To give light to an *A*,
Warmth to a *C*,
And hope to an *F*.

Definition of a Test

A test is
a gallant struggle
to remember
what you can't forget
until you can forget.

Don't Tell Me

Don't tell me
I won't fail,
For it might
Not be true,

Just tell me
You'll still
Love me,
Even if I do.

The Tragic Night

Bloom! Bloom!
I was supposed to bloom
When the lights shone
On my side of the room!

I was a tulip,
In our class spring play,
My part was to bloom,
When lights shone my way.

All of the flowers
Were curled up so tight,
On one side of the stage,
In the dark of night.

Bloom! Bloom!
I was supposed to bloom
When the lights shone
On my side of the room!

I waited
For those lights to say,
Flowers, bloom,
It's a splendid day!

I didn't open my eyes
Or even take a glimpse,
But it took so long that
My whole body grew limp.

> *Bloom! Bloom!*
> *I was supposed to bloom*
> *When the lights shone*
> *On my side of the room!*

I started to hear
Such a soft, dreamy tune,
Then I fell asleep,
In my flower costume.

> *And that's when the lights shone*
> *On my side of the room.*

All the tulips
So slowly rose,
Stretched their petals,
Began to grow,
Filled a garden
In perfect rows.

> But

One dumb flower
Stayed tucked up tight,
Didn't hear the sounds,
Didn't see the lights,
Didn't bloom at all,
That tragic night.

Bloom! Bloom!
I was supposed to bloom
When the lights shone
On my side of the room!

Two Eyes

Two eyes are buried
At the bottom
Of my bookbag.
I locked them
In a box
That looks like a coffin.

Then I covered it
Layer by
Sickening layer,
In two rolls
Of toilet paper
And placed
The horrid wad
In a black sock,
And hid it in
The deepest, darkest
Dungeon of my bookbag.

The eyes would have
Stayed there *forever*,
If only
My mother hadn't told
My teacher about them.

Ms. Digby just asked me
To read a sentence
From the blackboard,
And to tell her
If the commas
Are in the right place.

Commas?
I don't see any commas!

Now Ms. Digby
Is making me
Pull out the black sock,
Unroll the coffin case,
Unlock the eyes,
Put them on,
And become

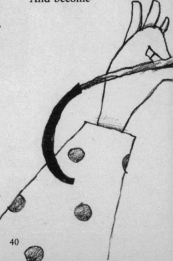

Four Eyes!

Wow! Ms. Digby!
I didn't know
You had freckles,
     Just like me!

Why Must It Be
Minus Three?

When I had
Three wrong
Out of twenty,
My teacher wrote
− 3

But that's like crying
When a few weeks
Of the summer holidays are over,
Instead of rejoicing
Because there are so many left,

Or fretting
About the cupcakes
With rainbow sprinkles
That have been eaten,
Instead of admiring

The luscious ones
Still waiting on the plate.

I think my teacher
Should have written

+ 17

Squirt! Squirt!
On the Teacher's Skirt
(Cast: Jimmy, Danny, Teacher)

Jimmy whispers to Danny:

> Let's forget our work today,
> Let's have a good time in here,
> Let's just goof off and play.

Danny whispers to Jimmy:

> I have to finish my math,
> And study all the new words,
> For our next spelling class.

Jimmy whispers to Danny:

> Spelling's a terrible bore,
> You practice a trillion words,
> And there's still a zillion more.

Danny whispers to Jimmy:

> Spelling is sure a pain,
> But I'll get detention,
> If I fail my test again.

Jimmy whispers to Danny:

> We need to have some fun.
> When the teacher doesn't look,
> I'll squirt my water gun.

SQUIRT! SQUIRT!
ON DANNY'S SHIRT

Danny whispers to Jimmy:

> Quick, give me a turn.
> My spelling is on fire,
> And I can't let it burn.

SQUIRT! SQUIRT!
ON ALL HIS WORK

Jimmy whispers to Danny:

> Return that gun to me!
> My pencils are exploding,
> It's time to fight or flee!

SQUIRT! SQUIRT!
WITH A GIANT SPURT

Danny whispers to Jimmy:

> My desk is all in flames,
> Quick, give me the water gun,
> I love this crazy game.

SQUIRT! SQUIRT!
Oh, no!
ON THE TEACHER'S
SKIRT

Teacher whispers to Danny:

> I'll take that toy away,
> And put your name on the blackboard
> For detention today.

Danny whispers to himself:

> So here we go again,
> Jimmy's bright ideas,
> And my detention!

If My Hand Didn't Get So Tired

I'd keep sixty journals and
Diaries,
And write all my friends'
Biographies.

If my hand didn't get so tired.

I'd have hundreds of pen pals
Overseas,
In countries from China to
Italy.

If my hand didn't get so tired.

I'd become a
Celebrity,
Writing sitcoms and movies for
TV.

If my hand didn't get so tired.

I'd write an entire
Library,
A zillion books,
All by me.

If my hand didn't get so tired.

I'd be the greatest writer
In history,
Known throughout
Eternity.

If my hand didn't get so tired.

My Writing Is an Awful Mess

My writing is an awful mess,
And my teacher asked me why.
"I zoom through my assignments,"
I told her with a sigh.

"I want to finish all this work,
So I can yack with friends,
I simply cannot wait until
The school day finally ends.

"I never check my spelling and
Punctuation, I don't try,
For if I spent my time on these,
My . . . social life would die.

"It's talking with my friends each day
That keeps my whole world bright,
And I don't want to give this up,
Just to get my schoolwork right."

There's a Cockroach Lurking Inside My Desk
(Cast: Lucas, Ms. Knoll, Gloria)

LUCAS:	Help! Help!
(Jumping	Ms. Knoll! Ms. Knoll!
up and down	Call the principal,
at his desk)	And the pest control!
MS. KNOLL:	Stop jumping up and down,
	And tell me what you've found.
LUCAS:	There's a cockroach
	Lurking in my desk,
	I felt its legs—
	And they're quite grotesque!
	It ran and hid,
	Near my pencil case,
	I peeked again,
	And looked at its face!
	A cockroach!
	Such a horrid bug!
	Made a home in my desk,
	Oh, yuck!

MS. KNOLL: Really, Lucas,
You must calm down
And stop jumping
All around.

If there is a bug
Hiding in your desk,
Handle the problem,
Deal with the pest,
And do it in a positive way,
No yelling,
No screaming,
No fussing,
Today!

GLORIA: Lucas ran to the janitor
And said,

LUCAS: Come quick!
There's a horrid bug
You have to evict.

GLORIA: For the rest of the week,
We were scared to look,
In our desks, our lunches,
And under our books.
On Friday we heard
A ghastly scream,
And knew another
Cockroach was seen.

Ms. Knoll: (*Jumping up and down*)	Help! Help! Mary! Lucas! Blanche! Call the police! And an ambulance!

Cockroaches are lurking
In my desk drawer,
If I look again,
I'll surely find more.
I saw the horrid,
Bristly sight,
That gave me such
An awful fright.

Cockroaches,
Of all the horrid bugs,
Have made a home
In my desk,
Oh, yuck!

LUCAS: Really, Ms. Knoll,
You must calm down,
And stop jumping
All around.

If there are bugs
Lurking in your desk,
Handle the problem,
Deal with the pests,
And do it in a positive way,
No yelling,
No screaming,
No fussing,
Today!

GLORIA: Ms. Knoll went
Screeching down the hall,

MS. KNOLL: Janitor,
Come and get them all!

GLORIA: Now we're worried,
Because we know,
Bugs lay eggs,
Wherever they go!

I Never Had an *A* Before

Last night,
While I was asleep,
I dreamed my teacher said,
"Great work, Ron!
I knew you could do it!
You earned an *A*
On your science test!"

When I woke up,
The dream started
To sail away,
But I soared
After it,
And caught it
By its silvery white tail,
And held on
With all my might,
But it disappeared
Through my hands,
Like stardust,
And blew away.

"Come back!
Come back!"

I cried.

"Stay just a little more,
I never had an *A* before."

Not Anymore

"Do you have any brothers and sisters?"
The teacher asked the child,
Who was new,
In our country,
And our school.

He sighed so long we thought
He would never breathe again.
Then in a rush of words,
Like water going
Over the falls,
He said,

I used
    to
        but
            not
                anymore
                    because
                        they
                            were
                              killed
                              in
                              a
                              war.

They Only See the Outside

On the outside, I'm just Benjie,
Shortest boy in grade four,
Just a hiccup in this classroom
That everyone ignores.

DRAGON DAYDREAM

But if a dragon came,
And tried to eat our class,
I'd rush the children out,
Till I was at the last,
Then I'd fight that dragon,
With my trusty sword,
And I'd end his blazing furies,
So we'd be safe once more.

ROMEO DAYDREAM

I know that if I was picked
To act in Shakespeare's play,
I'd turn into Romeo,
In a most gallant way.
And at the tragic ending,
When "With a kiss I die,"
Everyone would be in tears,
Everyone would cry.

HOCKEY DAYDREAM

I know if I was given
Skates and a hockey puck,
And plopped on an icy rink,
With just a touch of luck,
Everyone would cheer me on,
"Look at Ben out there,
He's faster than a bolt of light,
Other team, beware!"

They only see the outside,
Not the inside part of me,
But what I'd give for the chance
To set the inside free.

If Kids Were Put in Charge of Schools

If kids were put in charge of schools
For just a little while,
We'd make a few changes to
A zesty, kidsy style.

JIM: We'd turn twenty rooms into
               An Olympic pool to swim,
               And when we tired of diving,
               We'd play soccer in the gym.

KATIE: We'd have pizza on sale,
               Every second of the day,
               And the fountains in the school,
               Would be filled with lemonade.

PETER: We'd have private offices
               In a QUIET zone,
               Where we could concentrate and
               Work in peace alone.

ALICIA: We'd have three big libraries
               With every comic book,
               Newspapers and magazines,
               And time to dream and look.

NICK: We'd have artists drawing pictures,
                 Comedians sharing jokes,
                 And classes outside,
                 Under the mighty oaks.

STANLEY: We'd chase the brightest leaves in fall,
                 Catch snowflakes on our tongues,
                 And when the wind called out to us,
                 We'd join it on the run.

If kids were put in charge of schools
For just a little while,
We'd make a few changes to
A zesty, kidsy style.

The Bugs Are Out

Jane went home with the chicken pox,
While Sue had a bloody nose,
Marcos cried when his stomach hurt,
And Jack threw up on his clothes.

There is no doubt,
The bugs are out,
They're striking kids
And teachers out!

Rick turned white and feeble,
And crawled down to the nurse,
While John's head was pounding,
So much he thought it'd burst.

Sarah's body shook with chills,
And rattled when she spoke,
While David answered questions
With a "Croak, croak, croak."

There is no doubt,
The bugs are out,
They're striking kids
And teachers out!

The bugs are surely winning,
Oh, that's the way it goes,
Kathy just discovered
One measle on her nose.

Ms. Hogan is fading
As fast as all the rest,
She's greener than the grass,
Another bug's success!

There is no doubt,
The bugs are out,
They're striking kids
And teachers out!

The janitor just ran by
With a bucket in his hand,
When the bugs get in our school,
He is *always* in demand.

But he'll *never* bring those buckets,
To help a kid like me,
Though my stomach's started aching,
And wants to disagree!

PUKE!
PUKE!

THERE IS NO DOUBT,
THE BUGS ARE OUT,
THEY JUST STRUCK
THIS KID OUT!!

But I Have Mr. Cratzbarg

I don't have a father.
I don't have a grandfather.
I don't even have an uncle.

But I have
Mr. Cratzbarg.

When he says,
"It's storytime,"
I feel as if someone
Is giving me
A gigantic lollipop.
Every word he says
Is a scrumptious lick
Of peppermint or licorice,
And I don't *ever* want
His voice to stop.

When he asks,
"What's up, Tom?"
I know he *really* cares
That I won the soccer game
Or that my mother
Finally got a new job.

When he pats me on the head,
I feel as soft
As the banana inside my lunch.

I don't have a father.
I don't have a grandfather.
I don't even have an uncle.

But I have
Mr. Cratzbarg.

Whose Thumb Is This?

Class, it's time to go home,
Make sure you have everything.

Sarah, your fingers
Are in the finger drawer.

Here's a toe.
Check your feet.
Is anyone
missing a toe?

Miguel, no wonder
You can't hear!
Your ears are on the bookcase.

Whose thumb is this?
Will someone
Please claim her thumb.

Pete, here's the neck
For your scarf.

We've lost a head!
Nobody can go home
Until we find
Pedro's head.

Tara, your behind
Is *behind* you!

Finally,
You have all your parts
Together,
And you look wonderful!
You may line up now.
Have a great weekend!

(*Class files out the door.*)

Oh, no!

Here's one last nose,
Now whose could it be?

Don't Read This Book, Whatever You Do!

(Teacher is sneaking peeks at her book
while she is talking to students.)

Caution!
Warning!
Alarm!

I am your teacher,
And I'm begging you,

Don't read this book,
Whatever you do.

It's as if I'm stuck
To it like glue.

Read it today
As I walked to school.

Forgot attendance,
Then book money, too.

Sneaked peeks, during math,
I confess, it's true.

Didn't eat my lunch,
Just read right through.

Now color the lakes
On your maps in blue.

I'll try to finish
Before gym at two.